POPCORN
POPCORN
de maíz
de maíz

written by **Floyd Stokes**

illustrated by **Stephanie Lewis**

inspired by **Madison Stokes**

translation by **Camille B. Quirin**

To my popcorns Dwayne, Tressimee, Devin, Madison and Olivia.
I can't wait to see what you turn into.
- F.S.

All my love to my husband Byron, and my two wonderful adult children, Nelson and Kiyona.
They have been nothing but a steady force of encouragement to me; I have been blessed.
- S.L.

POP!

POP!

POP!

No part of this publication may be reproduced in whole or part, or stored on a retrieving system, or transmitted in any form or by any means, electronic, mechanical, photocopying, recording, or otherwise, without permission of the publisher. For more information regarding permission, visit www.superreader.org.

A publication of
The Amercian Literacy Corporation for Young Readers.
Text copyright © 2009 by Floyd Stokes.
Illustrations copyright © by Stephanie Lewis.
Translation by Camille B. Quirin.
Graphic Design by Kimberly Isenhour.
First edition, 2009. All rights reserved.
ISBN 978-1-56592-197-9

nforced for Library use
ted in China

And one landed
on the floor

All of a sudden...

Y una cayó en el suelo

De repente...

a **bear** began to **roar**

un oso comenzó a rugir

Mom was popping popcorn
And one landed
on a stump

All of a sudden...

POP

POP

POP

Mamá preparaba palomitas de maíz

Y una cayó sobre un tocón

De repente...

a frog began to jump

un sapo comenzó a saltar

Mom was popping popcorn
And one landed
on a string

All of a sudden...

POP

POP

POP

Mamá preparaba palomitas de maíz

Y una cayó en una cuerda

De repente....

a monkey began to swing

un mono se comenzó a balancear

Mom was popping popcorn

And one landed
in the swamp

All of a sudden...

Mamá preparaba palomitas de maíz

Y una cayó en un pantano

De repente...

Mom was popping popcorn
And one landed
on a wall

All of a sudden...

POP

POP

POP

Mamá preparaba palomitas de maíz

Y una cayó en la pared

De repente...

a snake began to crawl

una serpiente se comenzó a arrastrar

an elephant began to shake

un elefante se comenzó a sacudir

a whale began to float

una ballena comenzó a flotar

a giraffe
began to dance

una jirafa comenzó a bailar

a **dog** began to **bark**

un perro comenzó a ladra

Mom was popping popcorn

And one landed
in the sky

All of a sudden...

Mamá preparaba palomitas de maíz

Y una cayó en las nubes del cielo

De repente...

un águila comenzó a volar

She came into the room,
so I had to go to bed.

De repente, mamá entro en mi cuarto,
y me tuve que ir a dormir